Locating and Evaluating Information on the Internet

Books in THE INTERNET LIBRARY *series*

Communicating
on the Internet
Paperback 0-7660-1743-5
Library Ed. 0-7660-1260-3

The History of the Internet
and the World Wide Web
Paperback 0-7660-1746-X
Library Ed. 0-7660-1261-1

Creating and Publishing
Web Pages
on the Internet
Paperback 0-7660-1744-3
Library Ed. 0-7660-1262-X

Locating and Evaluating
Information
on the Internet
Paperback 0-7660-1745-1
Library Ed. 0-7660-1259-X

THE INTERNET LIBRARY

Locating and Evaluating Information on the Internet

Art Wolinsky

Enslow Publishers, Inc.

40 Industrial Road   PO Box 38
Box 398   Aldershot
Berkeley Heights, NJ 07922   Hants GU12 6BP
USA   UK

http://www.enslow.com

Copyright © 1999 by Art Wolinsky

All rights reserved.

Library of Congress Cataloging-in-Publication Data

Wolinsky, Art.
    Locating and evaluating information on the Internet / Art Wolinsky.
        p. cm. — (The Internet library)
    Includes bibliography and references.
    Summary: Provides an overview of the Internet and discusses how to find information on it and evaluate the quality of that information, with an emphasis on the World Wide Web.
    ISBN 0-7660-1745-1 (pbk)
    ISBN 0-7660-1259-X (library ed.)
    1. Computer network resources—Evaluation Juvenile literature.
2. Internet searching Juvenile literature. [1. World Wide Web (Information retrieval system) 2. Internet (Computer network)]
I. Title II. Series.
ZA4201.W65 1999
025.04—dc21   99-20378
                                            CIP

Printed in the United States of America

10 9 8 7 6 5

To Our Readers: We have done our best to make sure all Internet addresses in this book were active and appropriate when we went to press. However, the author and the publisher have no control over and assume no liability for the material available on those Internet sites or on other Web sites they may link to. Any comments or suggestions can be sent by e-mail to comments@enslow.com or to the address on the back cover.

Trademarks:
Most computer and software brand names have trademarks or registered trademarks. The individual trademarks have not been listed here.

Cover Photo: Index Stock Photography, Inc./Eric Kamp

Contents

Introduction

This is my friend Web. He will be appearing throughout the pages of this book to guide you through the information presented here and to take you to a variety of Internet sites and activities. Web is also a reminder that there is always more to learn about the Internet.

▶ The Gold Rush

In 1849, gold was discovered in California. Thousands of people streamed westward in search of riches. A few struck it rich, but many more learned that finding gold was not as simple as putting a shovel in the ground and digging.

Gold is one of thousands of minerals found in the earth's crust. Gold is considered valuable, but finding it is not easy. Once you do find it, you must determine whether you have the real thing and the quality of your discovery. If you are not careful and skilled, you will think you are rich; however, you may soon learn that you have dug through tons of earth to discover only fool's gold.

In the 1990s the Internet made it possible for people to gather valuable information. In today's world, good information can be as valuable as gold. There are millions of tons of earth that yield their precious minerals to those who are skilled. The Internet also yields valuable information to those who know where to find it and how to determine its quality.

Just as anyone can swing a pick ax or wield a shovel, so can just about anyone use an Internet search tool. But knowing the basics of tool use does not ensure locating gold or quality infor- mation. Tool use is only the first step. Knowing where to dig, which tool to use when, and being able to evaluate the quality of what you dig up will determine your success at mining minerals or min- ing the Internet.

Finding Gold:
Finding valuable information on the Internet is like digging for gold, you have to know where to start.

This book will take you beyond simply finding information. It will get you familiar with the wide range of tools available to dig information from the hundreds of millions of Web pages on the World Wide Web. It will help you determine the best tools to use for the information you want to dig up, as well as the quality of the information you retrieve.

You do not need an Internet connection to benefit from the information provided here, but searching is something that requires practice. If you have access to the Internet, you should be familiar with the World Wide Web and the use of your Web browser. With a connection, you will be able to practice the techniques offered and visit the sites my friend Web suggests.

Chapter 1

Searches on the Internet

Many people refer to the Internet as the world's largest library. Though there are similarities, there are also many differences, especially when you compare the Internet to school libraries. Probably the biggest differences are the amount of information, the reliability of information, and the variety of information available.

No one knows exactly how many Web pages exist on the Internet. I have heard estimates of over 400 million, and that is only on the World Wide Web. It is said that the total amount of information in the world doubles every two years. If the Web were to grow at the same rate, we could expect over 3 billion pages eventually. There are thousands of programs available to download, millions of additional pages of information in databases, and thousands of mailing lists, newsgroups, and other sources of online information. There is so much information that it can sometimes be overwhelming, and even inaccurate. (We will talk more later about the accuracy of information on the Internet.)

▶ A Note of Caution

The third difference between libraries and the Internet deals with the variety of information available. Libraries do not usually carry illegal information, pornography, or literature that promotes hate, drug use, or other antisocial activities; however, all of this information can be found on the Internet. Although you may not intend to look for this kind of material, there is a good chance that you could run into it while you are doing research on other appropriate topics.

It is your responsibility to be aware of this type of material and to know what to do when you come across it. If you find questionable material while doing research, it is best to simply click off of it and go on with your work. If you are disturbed, upset, puzzled, or curious about anything you come across online, do not hesitate to talk about it with your parents or your teachers. They can help you understand it and teach you how to deal with it in the future.

▶ Exponential Growth of Knowledge

What we find on the Internet represents just a small fraction of the total knowledge in the world.

| Internet Addresses | Information Facts | On Your Screen |

Along with discussing things with your parents and teachers, there are a few simple rules you should follow when visiting Web sites or when dealing with people on the Internet. You can read more about Internet safety at the following Web sites:

The Safe Kids Home Page
   <http://www.safekids.com>

Captain Jack's Safety Page
   <http://www.ventriloquist.net>

Cyberangels: The Largest Internet Safety Organization
   <http://www.cyberangels.org/>

On Your Screen

You can find out more about Internet safety at sites like this one.

If that seems like a lot of information, consider this: The total knowledge base in the world is doubling every three years. Think about that for a moment, then we will do some simple math to see what that means to you.

Let's make believe that we can fit all the knowledge in the world on a single sheet of paper, including those 400 million Web pages. How many pieces of paper will you have by the time you reach age ninety (the average life expectancy of today's seventh grader)? Stop here and see whether you can figure it out. Then, read on to check whether you were on target with your answer.

Let's assume that you are twelve years old and that you have the sheet of knowledge in front of you. Start by determining your life expectancy: Subtract your age from ninety (90 − 12 = 78). Next, divide your life expectancy by three to see how many times knowledge will double in your lifetime (78 ÷ 3 = 26). In this example, knowledge will double twenty-six times in your lifetime. Now, that is *not* twenty-six pieces of paper; knowledge *doubles* twenty-six times. Look at the following chart to see how many sheets of paper you would have.

With knowledge growing so rapidly, simply learning facts without knowing what to do with them is not going to give you a good education. You can never learn enough, and much of what you would learn is quickly outdated. Education today is

Internet Addresses   **Information Facts**   On Your Screen

If we assume all the knowledge in the world fits on one sheet of paper, this chart shows how many sheets of paper are needed to represent all of the knowledge in the world, doubling twenty six times.

1 = 2		14 =	16,384
2 = 4		15 =	32,768
3 = 8		16 =	65,536
4 = 16		17 =	131,072
5 = 32		18 =	262,144
6 = 64		19 =	524,288
7 = 128		20 =	1,048,567
8 = 256		21 =	2,097,152
9 = 512		22 =	4,194,304
10 = 1,024		23 =	8,382,608
11 = 2,048		24 =	16,765,216
12 = 4,096		25 =	33,530,432
13 = 8,193		26 =	67,060,864

not about learning facts. It is about learning how to find what you want when you want it and what to do with it once you have found it.

▶ Whom Do You Trust?

If you go into any library, you will find information on just about any area of human interest. The information, though not always accurate, had to pass some standards before it was published and placed on the library shelves. For example, Internet experts, editors, and proofreaders all read this book before it went to print. Then your librarian decided to purchase the book and probably reviewed it before putting it on the shelf. That process helped establish the reliability of the information in the book.

Reliable Information: To make sure this book was full of reliable information, a lot of people spent time researching it and checking the facts.

On the Internet, however, anyone can publish anything they want, anytime they want, without having to be approved by anyone. People are free to publish inaccurate information or even total lies. Today, this is a major problem facing people accessing information on the Internet.

With the Internet, as in other areas of your life, you have to learn not only how and where to locate information, but also how to determine whether the information is accurate and reliable.

Chapter 2

Searches Before the Web

In the early days of the Internet, it was difficult to even get online. You needed a good deal of computer knowledge, and you needed to know exactly which files you were looking for. There were no easy ways to search.

Let's take a quick look at two search tools that were used in the early days of the Internet and see how they compare with two search tools you might use today.

When the Internet was first created, files were sent from one computer to another by using a text-based set of commands for file transfer protocol (FTP). The main search tool was named Archie, but it was not something a novice could easily use.

Gopher, a user-friendly way of indexing files and information, was invented in the late 1980s. As a result, people began to see the Internet as a great place to dig for information. A new search tool named Veronica was also invented to search Gopherspace.

Today, the World Wide Web offers a great selection of search tools. We will take a quick peek at Yahoo and Infoseek, two of the original World Wide Web search tools. Later, we will examine these and other search tools more closely. Their power and ease of use had a big role in starting the information gold rush.

Since we have been speaking about the gold rush, let's go back and take a look at how we would go about finding information about the gold rush by using some of the previously mentioned tools.

▶ Archie

In the early days of the Internet, you could go to Archie if you knew the name of the file you wanted to retrieve. After typing in the file's name, you would be provided with a list of computers on the Internet that had that file available.

Archie is still around, but you must know how to use Telnet, one of the older Internet tools, to access many of the Archie servers. Telnet is still used in older systems. Fortunately, Archie and many of the other older search tools have been brought to the World Wide Web and can now be used with greater ease through your Web browser.

Let's take a look at an Archie search tool at <http://www.broward.cc.fl.us/cgi-bin/archie.pl>, on the following page. It is located on a computer at Broward Community College in Florida. It will actually search an Archie server in a part of the country closest to you.

The first thing you might notice is that I typed the term *goldrush* as a single word. I did this because Archie is a tool that was designed before spaces could be used in names. I might have to do three or four different searches to get results. I could also search for *gold_rush*, *gold-rush*, or simply *gold*.

You will also notice that I put a dot

Confused?
Some of the older search tools are a little difficult to use. Thankfully, it's a lot simpler to use the Internet now.

On Your Screen

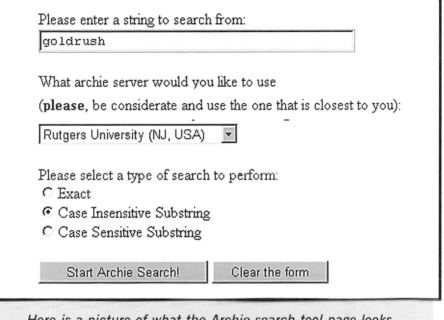

Please enter a string to search from:

goldrush

What archie server would you like to use

(**please**, be considerate and use the one that is closest to you):

Rutgers University (NJ, USA)

Please select a type of search to perform:
○ Exact
◉ Case Insensitive Substring
○ Case Sensitive Substring

Start Archie Search! | Clear the form

Here is a picture of what the Archie search-tool page looks like on your Web browser.

in the box next to "Case Insensitive Substring." I did this to indicate that, because I do not know the exact file name, I also do not know what the capitalization of it will be. This combination of words and search limitations will result in the maximum number of hits returned by Archie.

Unfortunately, regardless of which search I chose, Archie would not return any useful information about the 1849 gold rush. This lack of useful information comes as a result of the fact that Archie was used primarily to find computer software rather than text files. When someone wanted to find a piece of software, they usually knew at least part of the name, and Archie could do the rest.

During the early days of the Internet, software exchange was an important function of FTP. Some information was exchanged, but it was often between scientists and researchers who were working together on projects and knew what they were looking for and where to go to find it.

▶ Veronica

Gopher was introduced in the late 1980s as a user-friendly way of indexing documents. This new system allowed users to move through a series of menus until they located their desired document. However, each Gopher had its own collection of

| Internet Addresses | Information Facts | On Your Screen |

There are quite a few Archie tools that you can use to explore the "good old days." A few are listed below. Each of these is on a server in a different country, but the same person wrote all of them. Sharing was, and still is, a great part of the Internet.

<http://web.bilkent.edu.tr/archie.html>

<http://www.medcor.mcgill.ca/archie.html>

<http://www.dkrz.de/info/archie.html>

The country in which a server is located can often be determined by looking at the last two letters on the computer name. For example "tr" stands for Turkey, "ca" stands for Canada, and "de" stands for Germany.

Check the following site for a list of the two-letter abbreviations for all countries:

<http://www.aresearchguide.com/countrycode1.html>

information, and going from Gopher to Gopher was not an efficient way to search for information.

Veronica was a tool that searched all Gophers and returned information. However, it did not search entire documents. It only searched for the title of a document or for Gopher directories. To access Veronica, you could visit any Gopher and do a Veronica search from the Gopher menu. Today, it is difficult to find a Veronica search tool that is still functioning. I was fortunate to find one Web-based gopher site where I searched for information on the gold rush.

The search resulted in 516 files being returned, but most of them had nothing to do with the California gold rush because the search found articles containing *either* word.

To improve the search, I had to search for gold and rush. The *and* is a special search term understood by the software. It is called a Boolean term. We will learn more about Boolean searches later.

This time, the search returned six hits, four of which had to do with the California gold rush:

- 93-137 (a 1925 version of the Charlie Chaplin film *The Gold Rush*, restored)

- "The California Gold Rush and Black Immigration" by Elena Albert; interviewed by Elsa Knight Thompson

- California Gold Rush

- Umbeck, John R. (1977), "A Study of the California Gold Rush"

Where's my file?
Sometimes, when you search for information on the Internet, you may not find exactly what you want. You may have to try a new search.

- California Gold Rush
- "JOHNSON—The Second Gold Rush: Oakland and the East Bay in World War II"

As you can see, digging for information was not a simple matter in the early days, and it did not exactly resemble a gold rush of information. Luckily, over time searches got easier.

Chapter 3

Searches Become More User-Friendly

With the introduction of the World Wide Web, search tools took on a new look. They had a GUI interface. GUI is pronounced "GOOEY" and it stands for graphical user interface. A GUI interface uses a mouse along with point-and-click menus and icons instead of text and typing commands.

(You may think that I made a mistake when substituting the words for the acronym GUI, since the phrase *GUI interface* would read "graphical user interface interface." Technically you are correct, but *GUI interface* is the common phrase. It is like the Sahara Desert. The word *Sahara* means "desert." When you say *Sahara Desert* you are actually saying *Desert Desert*.)

Two new types of search tools emerged: the search index and the search engine. In Chapter 4 we will take a closer look at them, but for now we will simply examine the results of searching for gold rush information and compare them with the early search tools.

▶ The Early Indexes of the World Wide Web

Yahoo <http://www.yahoo.com> was one of the first search indexes. It is still the number one search index on the Internet. Unlike a search engine, which brings back a list of sites based on key words the user supplies, a search index is a series of choices the user makes in order to reach the information. In the next chapter Web will point you to other search engines, but we can take a quick look at the results of searching for gold rush information using Yahoo.

Moving through the different levels of categories, our search results in nineteen hits, or sites that match our search, thirteen of which are related to the California gold rush. The search index allows us to get more information without having to know about spaces in file names or Boolean terms.

If we visit the hits returned by Yahoo, we find that the amount of information returned is also greater than Archie or Veronica searches, and more of it relates directly to the gold rush.

▶ The Early Search Engines

Search engines compile large databases of information. One of the first search engines on the Web was Go Search Engine <http://www.go.com>. When I

Without the right search engine, finding something on the Internet can take longer than finding all of the toys in my house.

conducted a search for the gold rush on Infoseek, the top of the page read: **"Infoseek found 2,145,479 pages containing at least one of these words: gold rush."** Whoa! There were over 2 million pages, but many had just the word *gold* and many had just the word *rush*. Obviously there were many useless pages because the search engine looked for sites containing either the term *gold* or *rush*.

When we examine the first twenty hits, we find that thirteen of them deal with the California gold rush. That is good, but we can instruct the search engine to bring back only hits where the term gold rush appears as a phrase. Even better, I can tell it to bring back Web pages where the phrase *California gold rush* appears. When I do that, this is what I see at the top of the page. **"Infoseek found 1,867 pages containing the word 'California gold rush.'"** That certainly narrowed things down. If we scan the first twenty hits, we find that every single one seems to be related to the California gold rush.

Because computers compile and create the listings for the search engines, you can dig up many articles many different ways. For instance, suppose I wanted to find out about women in the gold rush. I could type in three key words: *women gold rush*. The search engine then looks for any of these words, because I did not tell it to do otherwise. As a result, it found more than 5 million articles, but look at the title of the first one: "Women of the Klondike."

Do not worry if you get thousands or even millions of hits. Many are duplicate entries, and you usually will not have to

Too Much:
Sometimes a search will result in too much information. That can be just as frustrating as not finding enough.

go past the first few screens to find what you need. If you do not find what you need in the first few pages, you should try the search again, using different search terms.

You may think that I was lucky it was the first entry, rather than the millionth, but luck had little to do with the organization of the search results. Search engines always attempt to present the articles they feel best match your search terms. They assume words that appear many times and close together are more likely to be what you are seeking, and they present them first on the list.

When you start to gain skill at selecting good search terms, you will find you may get hundreds, thousands, or millions of hits, but you will seldom have to look beyond the first few screens to find useful titles. Useful titles do not necessarily mean useful information, though. Keep in mind that you have to determine the quality of the information retrieved by the search engine.

Later, we will talk about evaluating information, but first we must concentrate on finding information to evaluate.

Chapter 4

Today's Search Tools

Although dozens of different types of search tools exist, we will group them into three different categories: search engines, subject trees (commonly known as search indexes), and meta search tools. Because most search tools are search engines, many people refer to subject trees and meta search tools as search engines.

Briefly, here are the major differences between the three types of tools.

- *Subject trees* are almost always created by people who visit Web sites and catalog the contents of the sites.

- *Search engines* are computer programs that go out to the Web each night and look for pages they have not visited. The computer program creates the index.

- *Meta search tools* are actually programs that search a number of search engines at the same time.

Because subject trees are cataloged by humans, they are unable to access the great number of Web pages that a search engine can. Thus, subject tree searches often result in fewer pages being returned as matches. However, what they lack in quantity, they often make up in quality, especially if you are looking for general information or places to start learning about a topic. Though the number of hits may be smaller, the information may be better. The better quality of information is a result of the fact that indexers are very particular about what they put in their indexes.

When a search engine visits a page, however, it indexes the page but does not evaluate the information. Therefore, your search could return a Web page devoted to painting your toenails gold rather than to information on the gold rush. That is not the case with a subject tree. Because the page is visited by a person, he or she would probably choose not to include the golden toenail page as part of the index.

Different search tools contain different information. Some may be better at finding business-related or historical information; others may be better at finding scientific information. As you experiment, you will probably settle on one or two search tools you will use for the majority of information. Others will become backup tools you will visit when information is scarce.

Me Web . . . King of the Internet: Climbing through an Internet search tree can be just as difficult as climbing a real tree.

Internet Addresses | Information Facts | On Your Screen

Here are a few subject trees (search indexes):

Yahoo   <http://www.yahoo.com>
Netscape Netcenter   <http://home.netscape.com/>
Nerd World   <http://www.nerdworld.com/>
World Wide Web Virtual Library
                            <http://www.vlib.org>

On Your Screen

```
WWW Virtual Library - Netscape                                    _ 8 X
File  Edit  View  Go  Communicator  Help
```

The WWW Virtual Library

- **Agriculture**
  Agriculture, Beer & Brewing, Gardening...

- **Computer Science**
  Computing, Languages, Web...

- **Communications and Media**
  Communications, Telecommunications, Journalism...

- **Education**
  Education, Cognitive Science, Libraries, Linguistics...

- **Engineering**
  Civil, Chemical, Electrical, Mechanical, Software...

- **Humanities**
  Anthropology, Art, Dance, History, Museums, Philosophy...

- **Information Management**
  Information Sciences, Knowledge Management...

- **International Affairs**
  International Security, Sustainable Development, UN...

- **Law**
  Law, Environmental Law...

- **Business and Economics**
  Economics, Finance, Transportation...

- **Recreation**
  Recreation, Games, Gardening, Sport...

- **Regional Studies**
  Asian, Latin American, West European...

- **Science**
  Biosciences, Medicine & Health, Physics, Chemistry...

- **Society**
  Political Science, Religion, Social Sciences...

Mirrors: vlib.org (USA), Stanford (USA), Penn State (USA), East Anglia (UK) Geneva (CH), Geneva 2 (CH), Argentina.

About the VL | Alphabetical listing | VL keyword search | What's New

Last update March 21, 1999

```
Document: Done
```

The World Wide Web Virtual Library is an example of a subject tree (search index).

▶ Subject Trees (Search Indexes)

The first search tools to arrive on the World Wide Web were subject trees. Yahoo was the first major subject tree. Today, Yahoo is still based on the subject tree idea, but it has a search engine added for those who like to search a different way.

These search tools are referred to as *trees* because they start out with a major subject heading, then branch off into smaller related subjects, then to smaller and smaller subjects until you end up at the end of a branch and the information you are seeking.

On Your Screen

Arts & Humanities Literature, Photography...	**News & Media** Current Events, Newspapers, TV...
Business & Economy Companies, Finance, Jobs...	**Recreation & Sports** Sports, Travel, Autos, Outdoors...
Computers & Internet Internet, WWW, Software, Games...	**Reference** Libraries, Dictionaries, Quotations...
Education Universities, K-12, College Entrance...	**Regional** Countries, Regions, US States...
Entertainment Cool Links, Movies, Humor, Music...	**Science** Biology, Astronomy, Engineering...
Government Military, Politics, Law, Taxes...	**Social Science** Archaeology, Economics, Languages...
Health Medicine, Diseases, Drugs, Fitness...	**Society & Culture** People, Environment, Religion...

If you were to do a search using Yahoo, you would see categories such as these from which to choose.

▶ A Sample Subject Tree Search

If you have an Internet connection, you can visit one of the search trees that Web has shown you. In case you do not have a connection, we can go through a search using Yahoo to show you what you can expect.

Suppose you were going to do a report on cloning for your science class. You would first visit the Yahoo main page and look at the major categories.

Clicking on the "Science" link would take you to another page containing over fifty additional categories. One of those would be "Biology." Clicking on the biology link would lead you to another group where you could find "Genetics." There you would find a link to "Cloning." Clicking on that link would give you links to ten Web sites that hold a great deal of information about animal cloning. Likewise, a link to "Human Cloning" has an additional twelve links to loads of information on the subject.

This method of searching for material is easy to use. It resulted in a compact list of Web sites, but those Web sites had links to other Web sites. The result was a great deal of information on a general (and in this case popular) topic.

▶ Search Engines and Juggling

Unlike subject trees, search engines locate information from words that the user supplies. The user types in key words or phrases that help the search engine determine what information to retrieve. The search engine finds Web pages that match the search and presents them. What could be easier?

To answer my own question, learning to juggle might be easier than learning to effectively use a search engine. Most people can throw a ball into the air and catch it, and most people can find a search engine and type in a search.

If you want to get work as a juggler, however, you are going to have to get at least two more balls into the air, and you

A Simple Trick:
Learning to juggle three balls is probably easier than effectively using a search engine.

Internet Addresses   Information Facts   On Your Screen

Here are links to five of the major search engines as well as to some search engines that were designed specifically with kids in mind.

Hotbot   <http://hotbot.lycos.com>
Altavista   <http://www.altavista.com>
Excite   <http://www.excite.com>
Go Search Engine   <http://www.go.com/>
Google   <http://www.google.com>

Just for kids
Yahooligans   <http://www.yahooligans.com>
    (Search index and search engine)
Ask Jeeves for Kids   <http://www.ajkids.com/>
Awesome Library for Teens
    <http://www.neat-schoolhouse.org/student5.html>

had better know how to do some tricks with them. Similarly, if you want to locate information efficiently, you have to know how to use more than one search engine, and you have to be able to do a few tricks with them.

▶ Key Words—Throwing One Ball

All search engines allow you to search for information by using key words. Key words are words that describe your topic or are words you would expect to find within the Web pages you want to retrieve.

You could go to any search engine and type in the word *cloning*. That process is similar to throwing the first ball into the air when you juggle. If you run that search through four different search

On Your Screen

This is what you might see if you were to use HotBot's search engine.

engines, you would get between thirty-five thousand and two hundred sixty thousand hits. Because you used only one key word, every article had the word *cloning* in it. I might be lucky enough to find what I wanted in the first few pages, but it is probably a good idea if you help the search engine help you.

▶ Multiple Key Words—Throw Another Ball

By using more than one key word, I can eliminate many of the items that do not interest me. Let's assume that I want to find information about human cloning. Using the phrase *human cloning* at the same four search engines, I now get between 33,164 and 4,451,948 hits.

Does that surprise you? I bet you thought that adding the extra word would narrow the search and result in fewer, more accurate hits. The larger number of hits is easily understood if you that realize search engines handle the same search phrases differently. For example, when you type in the phrase *human cloning*, some search engines assume that you want pages that contain *both* of the words; other search engines assume that you want pages that contain *either* word. The different ways in which these search engines search explains why we end up with even more hits. To narrow our search, we now have to throw the third ball into the air.

▶ Boolean Searches

George Boole (1815–1864) was an English mathematician who created a system of logic that became the foundation of algebra, other higher math, and computer logic. He defined relations between numbers, from which decisions could be made. That relationship is brought to words and search engines.

If you want to find out more about George Boole, you can try using one or more of the major search engines. He would also make a great topic for a report or a math project.

In the meantime, we have to see what George Boole has to do with search engines. Search engines follow Boolean logic in their gathering of information. The problem of excessive hits returned has to do with something called the default search mode.

Computers often have two or more methods for accomplishing any given task. If you do not tell a computer which method to use, the computer programmer has selected one to be used automatically. This is called the default method. In other words, it is what the computer does if you do not give it other directions.

In the case of search engines, some use the *and* default for search terms; others use the *or* default. The easiest way to find out which method is used by a search engine is to visit the "help" or "tips" page found at every search engine. This page will not only give you the basic information you need, but also provide you with information you need to do a few juggling tricks.

Advanced Searches: Once you learn how to juggle some key words, finding things gets easier on the Internet.

There is no simple way to know what to type to make the search engine look for both key words. You have to learn how each engine works. For example, to search for information on human cloning on one search engine, you may have to type the phrase *human and cloning*. On another, you may have to type *+human +cloning*. In most cases, though, you need only type *human cloning*.

Figuring out how different search engines work may sound confusing, but you will probably find a favorite search engine or two for most of your work and will become skilled enough so that you will need to visit others only occasionally.

Chapter 5

Beyond the Basics

N ow that you have learned how to juggle, so to speak, you need to learn some tricks. With juggling, it does not matter which ball you throw into the air first; with searching, that is not always the case. Search engines usually give the most importance to the first word in the list of key words and less to each one after that. A search using the words *California* and *oranges* will often supply results different from one using the words *oranges* and *California*.

You can perform plenty of tricks once you learn the advanced search techniques that are available through each search engine. Some search engines make it easy for you to refine your search through the use of pull-down menus and forms. Often, it is these little features that help you decide which search engine will become your favorite.

Find What You Want: With the right tricks, you can find just about anything you are looking for on the Internet.

You can tell the search engine to look for certain words but to ignore them if they are found with other words. For example, if you were doing a report about Abe Lincoln and typed, *Lincoln NOT Nebraska*, some search engines would return only pages where the word *Lincoln* appears without the word *Nebraska*.

Some search engines allow you to

search different parts of the Internet, search for pictures or sounds, narrow searches by date or country, or search many other possible ways.

Regardless of which search engine you use, there is almost always a way to refine your search by using the advanced features. You can usually reach the advanced features through a button located near the search form submit button. It might be labeled *Advanced Searching*, *Additional Options*, *Hints*, *Tips*, *Help*, or something similar, but they all have ways to refine your search.

If all this seems confusing, do not worry about becoming a master juggler right away. You have plenty of time to learn and practice, and you probably will not need tricks for most of your searching. I know many of the tricks, but usually just searching for a phrase or key words gets the results I need.

▶ Making Sure You Are Not Ignored

Another problem you will face when using multiple search engines is the way they handle plurals and uppercase letters. If you are not careful, you may conduct searches that bring back only a fraction of the hits you want, or you may bring back more information than you want.

For example, if you were doing a search about man's best friend, you would need information about dogs. (By now you probably realize that you must narrow your search with more than just the word *dogs*, but we will do the search to make a point.)

You may get a different set of results from using the word *dog* than you would by using the word *dogs*. Different search engines handle the words differently. Here are some of the possibilities if you just use the word *dog*: One search engine might return all articles that contain the word *dog* but ignore the word *dogs*; another search engine might return any word that starts with the letters *d o g*.

Uppercase letters can also be a problem. Whereas some search engines ignore them, others use them to narrow a search. For example, if you typed the key word *Dog*, one search engine might ignore any match that does not start with an uppercase letter. It is a good idea to check the help, tips, or advanced search options on each search engine to see how it handles plurals and uppercase letters.

▶ Perfecting Your Juggling Act

Searching is a skill that takes practice. You may not always have success, but the more searches you do, the better you will get.

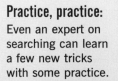

Practice, practice:
Even an expert on searching can learn a few new tricks with some practice.

I often ask my students to locate information, and they come back a little later saying, "There is not any information on that topic." In most cases there is plenty of information, but they just used the wrong search terms. You have to think of topics that mean the same as your unsuccessful search but use different words.

This exact situation once happened to me. A long time ago, long before the Internet, I did a social studies lesson in which my class and I discussed what would happen if all the cats in the United States were to disappear overnight. We discussed rat control, disease, cleanup, the economy, how we would handle the situation, and whether we would survive. We then discussed what would happen if all the cats in India were to disappear.

When I presented the original lesson more than twenty years ago, we had little information about India except for what we could find in the library and other books in school. Despite our lack of information, we had some great discussions, and students really had to think about real situations and how they would react.

I wanted to see what would happen with the same lesson today, using the Internet. The first thing I decided to do was to learn more about cats in India. I did a search, using the words *domestic, cats,* and *India.* I used these words in different orders and in different combinations, but I came up with very little information. Tigers were the only cats for which I could obtain any information.

I knew there had to be information about domestic cats, and figured I was using the wrong search terms. I began to think about the real topic, which in this case was basically rat control. When I used the words *rat control,* not only did I find information, I also found out something that took me completely by surprise.

Rat Control Problem?
I don't understand why people have a problem with rats. Hey, after all my best friend *is* a mouse.

Before I tell you what I found, if you have an Internet connection, you may want to stop reading, log on to the Internet, and see whether you can find information about cats or rat control in India. If you can locate the information, you will have an easy answer to the question, "What would happen if all the cats in India were to disappear tonight?"

▶ The Results

One of the articles I found was titled "The First No-Kill City." Here are a few lines that opened my eyes:

> Speeding out of the airport, a hired car dodges foraging street dogs. . . . Stray dogs are as ubiquitous as people sleeping on streets. There are no stray cats in sight. Perhaps the dogs kill them, a visitor thinks. Perhaps they can't survive the traffic, intense even this late. . . . Street dogs remain the first defense against rats and rat-carried disease. . . . Cats are so rarely kept as pets in India and are generally so scarce that

On Your Screen

The Internet has almost as many tools for searching as topics to search.

most cities don't even consider them an animal control problem.

So, the answer to the question is pretty simple. Nothing much would have happened because there are so few cats, and they are not the ones who control the rat population.

This one search, however, points out the need to think about your search terms and illustrates the power of the Internet to provide real information that has an impact on our lives.

▶ Meta Search Engines

The final type of search tool is called a meta search engine. This search engine actually searches other search engines. It is a good place to go if you are having a problem locating information by using single search engines.

Meta search engines have the advantage of being able to search many search engines at the same time, but you cannot do much in the way of advanced searching. Because there are marked differences between advanced searches, there is no

| Internet Addresses | Information Facts | On Your Screen |

These are some of the many meta search engines that you can explore:

InfoSpace:	\<http://www.metafind.com\>
Dogpile:	\<http://www.dogpile.com/info.dogpl/\>
Metacrawler:	\<http://www.metacrawler.com/ info.metac/dog/index.htm\>
Starting Point:	\<http://www.stpt.com/\>
Debriefing:	\<http://www.debriefing.com/\>
Highway 61:	\<http://www.highway61.com/\>
Verio:	\<http://search.verio.net/\>

way to create a meta search engine that will work on more than a few search engines. Meta search engines work on key words and usually allow the simple Boolean terms *and*, *or*, and *not*. However, because not all search engines use these expressions, even they may be ignored.

▶ The Next Generation

It is hard to keep up with changes in search engines. It seems a new one is always popping up or that one of the old ones is adding new features or a new look and feel. As search engines continue to develop and improve, the next generation will allow users to type in questions and phrases. They will make an attempt to understand plain English search phrases. Two of the major search engines have experimented with plain English versions, but neither was functioning at this writing. There are at least two other such search engines in existence today. One has a version especially for children.

Plain English search engines allow you to type in questions such as, "Who is Thomas Edison?" or "How do I fix my sink?" They react differently and bring back different results, depending on how you

Internet Addresses	Information Facts	On Your Screen

Here are some plain English search engines:

Ask Jeeves   <http://www.askjeeves.com/>

Ask Jeeves for Kids   <http://www.ajkids.com/>

Northern Light   <http://www.northernlight.com>

Internet Addresses Information Facts   On Your Screen

Although the major search engines offer a great deal of information, there is also plenty of information to be found in other places. Some of these are specialized search engines and others are searchable Web sites. The following sites have links to literally hundreds of other search engines:

All-in-One Search Page
   <http://www.AllOneSearch.com>
Cybersleuth Kids
   <http://www.cybersleuth-kids.com/>
Big Search Engine Index
   <http://www.search-engine-index.co.uk/>
Library Spot
   <http://www.libraryspot.com/>

phrase your questions. For example, "Who is Thomas Edison?" will bring back results different from "Why was Thomas Edison famous?"

Ask Jeeves has an interesting feature that presents users with a list of other related questions to which it knows the answer. This type of search engine shows a lot of promise and is fun to explore. However, it still has a long way to go before it really understands what you are asking.

Chapter 6

Using Information From a Search

O nce you are comfortable searching for information, you will find a wide range of information and sources for each topic you research, but that is only part of the job. How can you be sure the information you find is reliable and accurate? How do you know it is true?

Anyone can publish Web pages. There are people who want your money and make Web pages designed to sell you things. There are people who make pages because they want you to believe what they believe. There are people who make Web pages because they want your personal information to sell information to businesses. There are people who make Web pages because they want to share knowledge. They want you to become informed and educated.

Which pages must you read with caution and a questioning mind? The answer is simple: All of them! You would probably agree that advertising sites, biased or misleading sites, sites designed to promote hate, and information-gathering sites should all be carefully considered, but you might think it strange that a teacher would tell you to also carefully consider educational sites that want you to become informed.

It is often difficult to determine why a site is on the Internet. Propaganda and hate sites are often disguised as educational sitcs. They will tell you lies and use tricks to get you to think their way.

Advertising is often mixed in with educational material related to the product the Web creator is trying to sell. These sites often tell you only one side of the story to persuade you to buy their product.

Your name and other personal information are also valuable things on the Internet. People who gather information and compile mailing lists can make big money selling that information. These people will often provide information, entertainment, and contests as lures so that they may gather your personal information.

Keep it Secret:
Don't give out any personal information on the Internet without your parents' permission.

Even people who want to provide only information to you can mislead you. Not all information is true or accurate, and people with the best of intentions sometimes make mistakes. If they publish those mistakes and people believe them, they can do more harm than good.

So, the question is how do I find good, true, reliable information and how do I recognize it when I find it? The answer is to develop critical-thinking skills. Let's take a look at how you can begin judging the quality of the information you find.

▶ Columbus Sailed in *1493*?

While preparing a lesson on Columbus Day, I found Professor Hildegard Black's "Oddities of History" Web site. It had some strange and interesting facts. According to the site, "Columbus Day falls on October 12. History tells us Columbus landed in America on October 12, 1492, but did you know it was NOT 1492? It was really 1493!"

While Columbus was crossing the ocean, Portuguese scientists recalculated the calendar. They added three months. The king made it law BEFORE Columbus landed. When Columbus landed he thought it was October 12, 1492, but back in Portugal it was really January 12, 1943. He had a real shock when he landed in Portugal to report to Queen Isabella.

Isn't that an interesting set of facts? If you think so, do not go running to tell your history teacher just yet. It may be interesting, but it is also false. The Internet is full of wonderful, interesting, and incorrect information. I gave you wrong information to make a point. You cannot believe everything you read. Finding information is just part of your job.

If you found the errors in the Columbus story or doubted its truth as you read, you may be well on your way to being a critical thinker. If you

Some people on the Internet will intentionally try to mislead you with false information. Do not trust everyone, and try not to listen to these pirates.

believed it simply because it appeared in print, you may need to sharpen your critical-thinking skills.

Let's see what a critical thinker might do with Professor Black's information. A critical thinker might ask some of the following questions:

1. *Who printed the information?* Nowhere on the site did it tell anything about Professor Black. That does not mean the professor is not real, but without more information it is possible that the professor could be a fifth-grade student having some fun.

   I searched both HotBot and Four11 for Hildegard Black but could not find anything useful. A critical thinker would begin to doubt the information, but I still cannot say there is no professor or that the information is wrong.

2. *Is the person an expert?* How do you know? I found nothing to convince me that the professor is an expert or even a real professor.

3. *Is there a way to check on the author?* Do they have a phone number or an address? (An e-mail address is often not enough.) There was an e-mail address. Anyone can set up an e-mail account, using any user name he or she chooses. There was no other contact information. I did not have much faith in the professor at this point.

4. *Is the author trying to convince you of something? Are you getting all the facts or are some being withheld?* It seems as if the professor is expecting me to believe her odd facts, but she did not give me many details.

5. *Does the author state the source of the information or is it just his or her opinion?* There was no source of information mentioned. By

this point, neither the professor nor her information seems very credible.

6. *Can you find other sites with the same information?* I could not find any information about a calendar change in 1492 or 1493.

7. *Are there any obvious errors or things that do not add up?* Here is the point where good research and critical-thinking skills could have settled the question immediately. Since the object of research is to become well informed, the researcher should be learning about Columbus.

If you know about Columbus, you would know that he was born in Italy but sailed for Spain. When he returned, he did not land in Portugal. He landed in Spain, and Queen Isabella was the queen of Spain, not Portugal. Simply comparing the facts as presented in the article to ones you already know should have given you a clue.

Even if everything else was true, one misleading fact can throw doubt on all the accurate ones. There is a lesson here for those of you who are going to post information on the Internet. Make sure your facts are accurate.

Besides these obvious errors, there are other things that do not add up. For instance, if Portugal had recalculated the calendar, wouldn't everyone else in Europe also change their calendar? In that case, it would have been a major event in history, and we would be able to find information easily. If the rest of Europe did not change, today Portugal would

Truth? Or Lies?
Don't believe everything you read or see on the Internet, because some of it might not be true or real.

Critical thinking is not just something to be used on the Internet or for information gathering. It is a tool for life and a tool for all subjects. Here are some Web sites that you can visit to have fun and sharpen your critical-thinking skills.

The Just4Kicks Puzzle Page
<http://www.winn.com/j4k/>

Brain Teasers   <http://www.eduplace.com/math/brain>

BrainBashers   <http://www.brainbashers.com/>

If you think your critical-thinking skills are really sharp, you can visit Critical Thinking in Math From the Absurd Math Odyssey.

<http://www.learningwave.com/abmath/>

have a calendar different from the rest of Europe. I think it is safe to conclude that Professor Black's site is not a good one to use for research.

Are you starting to get the idea about critical thinking? Not all misleading information will be as easy to identify as this, but you have a basis to start the critical-thinking process.

Chapter 7

Misinformation and Misinterpretations

Did you try to find Professor Hildegard Black's "Oddities of History" Web site? If so, did you have any luck? If you were not able to find any information, did you think you were using poor search technique or did you begin to use critical thinking to question my example? If you *did* find the page, it may be because someone read this book and created it just to try to fool you. The fact is the Web site is pure fiction. It did not exist when I wrote this book. I made it up to illustrate my point. If you questioned it, good for you.

▶ Some Real Stories

The more research you do on the Internet, the more misleading information you are likely to find. Professor Black was not real, but all the Web sites and incidents that follow are. You can check them out if you like.

▶ Recruiting College Athletes

Two of my students were doing research on the recruiting of college athletes. They knew college athletes often get help gaining admissions to college, so they did a search, using the key words *athlete college entrance exam*. They were surprised at how many places had an example of a test and called me over to take a look. They asked me whether I had ever seen the test, and I told them I had. As I walked away, I heard one of them say, "I can't believe how easy it is!"

If you have an Internet connection, do a search, using those words. Examine what you find. I think you will find out why I had to fight to keep from laughing. Go ahead. Do the research before reading on. If you do not have an Internet connection, read on and I will explain. First read the initial questions of the test.

Internet Addresses | Information Facts | On Your Screen

Athletes College Entrance Exam
SU College of Arts & Sciences
ENTRANCE EXAM
COLLEGE ATHLETE VERSION
Time Limit: 3 weeks

1. What language is spoken in France?

2. Give a dissertation on the ancient Babylonian Empire with particular reference to architecture, literature, law, and social conditions.

   -OR-

   Give the first name of Pierre Trudeau.

3. Would you ask William Shakespeare to:
   a. build a bridge
   b. sail the ocean
   c. lead an army
   d. WRITE A PLAY

You should also realize that this page is not a real test—it is making fun of athletes. If you are an athlete, you probably do not think it is very funny. It could, however, just as easily be making fun of some other group of people. Pages that make fun of nationalities or groups of people are not in good taste. This is a form of prejudice, and you should recognize it as being inappropriate.

My students' comment about how easy the test was told me that they were not reading critically. The questions were easy because it was not a real test. Likewise, my students did not examine the test's Web site to see who or what group was the host. Apparently they did not even read the test carefully. Do you know of any test that has a three-week time limit?

▶ Election 1996

Before the 1996 presidential election, a friend of mine asked me to visit the Web sites created by her class. One student had created a Web site that listed all the major candidates running for president of the United States. As I scrolled down the list of Democratic candidates, I came across the name Patrick Paulsen and the following quote from the site:

> Perennial presidential candidate Pat Paulsen is the first aspirant to the oval office to run his campaign via the Internet. From his hillside home in California, Paulsen will not only keep the public and press advised of his own activities in behalf of the Democratic nod, but will answer "relevant" questions from prospective constituents, fans,

friends and opposing candidates by way of e-mail which he calls "yesterday's on ramp to the information super highway, tomorrow's Post Its."

I had to keep myself from laughing. It was obvious the student had done a good deal of research to find the different candidates. Unfortunately, it was equally obvious he had not evaluated the material at the Web sites he located, at least not at this one.

If you are not rolling on the floor, there is nothing wrong with your sense of humor (or mine). Neither the student nor the teacher was even born when Pat Paulsen ran for president for the first time in the 1968 presidential election.

If the student had taken the time to examine the contents of the site beyond the home page, he might not have recommended it. At the very least, he would have handled it differently.

If the Internet keeps getting more popular, maybe I'll be able to run for president in the next election. I would promise a mouse for every computer, and faster Internet connections for everyone. (But, remember, you can't believe everything you read. . . .)

You can visit what is left of the Pat Paulsen site. Today, there is just the home page with some missing graphics and broken links, but it is enough to give you an idea of what he saw. Here's the site:

<http://www.paulsen.com/>.

If you have an Internet connection, visit the site. Then do a little searching for information on Pat Paulsen and see if you figured out why I laughed so hard when I saw the name. Do not go on to the next section until you are ready to check whether you are correct.

▶ The Rebirth of a Candidate

By now you may have learned that Pat Paulsen is a comedian who was a regular on the *Smothers Brothers Comedy Hour*, a hit television show in the 1960s. The first time that Paulsen ran for president was as a weekly comedy sketch during the 1968 season. The Internet offered him an opportunity to get in front of an audience again, and the Web site was his stage.

▶ So What's the Big Deal?

You may not think this is a big deal, but the simple fact is that you must always be careful about information you retrieve or you might be misinformed. Similarly, you must be careful of what you post so that you do not misinform others. In this case, all of the student's hard work was questioned because he published an error that suggested a lack of careful research.

▶ Getting Serious

All these examples are meant to be humorous, but there is plenty of information on the Internet that is intended to provide false, damaging, and sometimes hateful information. There are hate groups who believe they are superior to others. They promote hate and violence through the use of lies, propaganda, and tricks that appeal to your emotions.

It is one thing to use these types of tricks to get you to make a purchase; it is something entirely different to use these tricks to get you to hate someone, to commit a crime, or to participate in an act of violence.

| Internet Addresses | Information Facts | On Your Screen |

There are not many sites on the Internet that have information that is easy for young people to understand. Here are three that will teach you about misleading information and hate groups. I suggest having your parents or teachers help you with these sites. They may be somewhat difficult to understand, but media awareness is a serious subject that deserves your effort.

Propaganda Analysis
   http://www.propagandacritic.com/>

Media Awareness
   <http://www.media-awareness.ca/eng/>

Southern Poverty Law Center
   <http://www.splcenter.org>

If you learn about how words can be used to persuade people to do things, you will be arming yourself against these hate sites. You may even save yourself a few dollars when you learn how companies are getting you to spend money on expensive brands and getting you to buy things you do not really need.

▶ Evaluating the Quality of Information

When visiting a Web site, the first thing you should do is read the material and ask yourself whether it makes sense. Is there information you question? Does information seem to be missing? Answering yes to any of these questions is an indication the information may not be reliable. Here are some questions to ask and things to look for that will help you decide on the usefulness of the information:

1. Who created the page? Was it an unidentified person, or is there an e-mail link to communicate with the author? What makes this person an expert?

2. Was the page created by an organization? If so, what is the purpose of the organization?

3. What is the purpose of the page, and who is the audience?

4. Does the author tell you the source of the information so that you can verify it? Is there a bibliography?

5. Is the information current?

6. Are there links to other reliable sites that contain information that can verify *their* information?

Chapter 8

Creating a Quality Product

You will most likely conduct research because you must create a project, report, or presentation for school. Often, adults must go through the same process in their jobs. Finding and evaluating information is a critical process, but it is only half of your job. You must collect pieces of information, understand what they mean, and then put them together to make a presentation of some kind. The presentation could be a written paper, a play, artwork, a Web site, or any other form of presentation that shows what you learned or presents information you want others to understand and value.

After you have judged the quality of information you found, you create a presentation. Now, others will judge the quality of the information you provide. If you want to create projects that people will value, it is important to take the proper steps leading up to the presentation.

There are some basic things to keep in mind if you really want a quality product. Whatever you create must be your work. Copying and pasting information to create a report is not an acceptable way of doing things for three major reasons.

First, it is almost impossible to put together pieces of articles from many different sources in a way that makes sense. A written project must have a logical beginning, middle, and end. The information should flow smoothly from one part to the other.

Second, taking the words and thoughts of other people without giving them credit is actually a form of stealing. Stealing someone's words is called plagiarism. As you advance through school, plagiarism is considered a very serious offense. It can cause you to fail a paper or even a course. Recently a congressman had his career seriously damaged because he plagiarized parts of a speech.

Finally, doing work by copying and pasting information does not put your mind through the process of learning how all the pieces fit together and have meaning. In other words, you do not really learn much and you waste a great deal of your time.

▶ The Research Process

The process of preparing a paper or Web site is not difficult. The steps leading up to the product are very similar for many types of research. If you practice them, they will become good habits that will serve you well for the rest of your life.

I cannot provide you with the details of creating a full research project, but I can provide you with an overview. Your teachers will provide you with the details. Here are some basic steps in the research process:

1. *Form a question or solve a problem.* Your question should be one that challenges your mind. There may be no one correct answer. Your job is to convince your readers that your answers are good ones. Let's use the example of cloning. It is tempting and easy to gather a

bunch of facts and create a report titled "Cloning," but this is not going to be a valuable experience for you and may not be an interesting topic for your readers.

It is much more challenging to do research to answer the question "How can cloning help wipe out world hunger?" Even better, you might choose to solve a problem and create a project titled "A Blueprint to Wipe Out World Hunger Through Cloning." Which report would you rather read?

2. *Locate sources of information.* Use search engines, books, magazines, experts, and any other source of information you can find. The more sources and the greater the variety, the better.

3. *Read your information and take notes.* Note taking is often in the form of copy and paste. As you visit a Web page or do other types of electronic research, you can copy from your source and paste it into a word-processing document. Make sure to include notes detailing where you found your information. You will need that information when you create your bibliography.

4. *Sort, sift, and organize your notes.* Once you have taken notes, you must read through them, determine how they relate to each other, and organize them so that they begin to form a picture of your product.

5. *Draft your project.* Once you have a clear picture of how everything fits together, you can

Stealing is Wrong: You can get in trouble for stealing someone else's words or ideas and trying to pass them along as your own. Don't do it.

begin drafting your project. A good project will have an introduction that presents the question or problem to be solved. Then the reader must be provided with whatever information they need to understand the problem or question and your arguments. The closing of the project should summarize the material that came before it and offer convincing solutions or answers.

6. *The project should include most of the following items*:

Citations—If you are going to use someone's exact words, you must give that person credit. This is done through citations that give credit to the authors. Your school might have a special way for you to write Internet citations. Check with your teachers. Here are some other places to look for citation information:

<http://www.columbia.edu/cu/cup/cgos/idx _basic.html> (Columbia University Press)

<http://www.bedfordstmartins.com/guide-book/online_6a.htm> (Axelrod/Cooper: A Writer's Guidebook)

<http://www.religioustolerance.org/int_cita.htm> (ReligiousTolerance.org)

Bibliography—This is a list of all your sources of information.

Glossary—This provides definitions to terms used in the project. This section is optional, but if you are doing a project that contains terms the reader may not be familiar with, it is a good idea to include a glossary.

▶ Summing Up

In this book we started out by learning about the history of searching. Then we learned about how to actually locate information. From there we went on to talk about the importance of evaluating what you find and provided you with ideas of how to go about determining the quality of information you locate. Finally, we talked about how you can use what you have found to make a quality presentation.

The early gold diggers needed tools and skills to find gold. The same is true of mining the Internet for information. The search engines are your basic tools. Refining searches, using Boolean searches, and knowing which search engines to use for your questions will develop your skills and make information location and retrieval much easier.

May all the information you mine on the Internet be as valuable as gold.

See You Later . . .
Well, it's been fun, and we sure learned a lot about how to find and evaluate information on the Internet. I can't wait to do some more Internet surfing! See you soon!

Glossary

Boolean algebra—George Boole, an English mathematician, developed this mathematical system which is used to solve problems in logic, probability, and engineering. Boole's system shaped the development of computer logic and computer languages.

default search mode—The method by which a computer automatically accomplishes a task. In other words, it is what a computer does if the user does not give it other directions to follow.

file transfer protocol (FTP)—A text-based set of commands that help different computers to communicate with each other.

Gopher—A user-friendly way of indexing files and information. It was introduced in the late 1980s, and allows users to move through a series of menus until they locate their desired document.

Infoseek—One of the two original World Wide Web search tools. (Yahoo is the other.)

key words—Words used in a search for information on the Internet. The words either describe the topic or are words that one would expect to find within the Web pages to be retrieved.

meta search engines—Programs that search a number of search engines at the same time. In other words, they are search engines that actually search other search engines.

propaganda—Information or ideas that are spread deliberately to try to influence the thinking of other people. Often propaganda is untrue or unfair.

search engine—A tool that compiles large databases of information and brings back a list of sites based on key words that the user supplies.

search index—A tool that enables the user to make a series of choices to reach the desired information.

Veronica—A search tool that was invented to search Gopherspace.

Yahoo—One of the two original World Wide Web search tools. (Infoseek is the other.)

Further Reading

Computers and Children. Charleston, S.C.: Computer Training Clinic, 1994.

Henderson, Harry. *The Internet*. San Diego, Calif.: Lucent Books, 1998.

The Internet: How to Get Connected and Explore the World Wide Web, Exchange News and E-mail, Download Software, and Communicate On-Line. New York: D K Publishing, Inc., 1997.

McCormick, Anita Louise. *The Internet: Surfing the Issues*. Springfield, N.J.: Enslow Publishers, Inc., 1998.

Mitchell, Kim. *Kids on the Internet: A Beginners Guide*. Grand Rapids, Mich.: Instructional Fair, 1998.

Moran, Barbara, and Kathy Ivens. *Internet Directory for Kids & Parents*. Foster City, Calif.: IDG Books Worldwide, 1998.

Index